MOTOWN FROM
THE OTHER SIDE

Motown From The Other Side

Remember All Things
Are Possible To Those
Who Believe!

Mark 9:23

FRANCES (FRAN HEARD) MACLIN

Frances (Fran Heard) Maclin

Library of Congress Control Number:		2021921710
ISBN:	Hardcover	978-1-6641-9600-1
	Softcover	978-1-6641-9599-8
	eBook	978-1-6641-9598-1

Scripture quotations marked KJV are from the Holy Bible, King James Version
(Authorized Version). First published in 1611. Quoted from the KJV Classic
Reference Bible, Copyright © 1983 by The Zondervan Corporation.

Print information available on the last page.

Rev. date: 10/23/2021

To order additional copies of this book, contact:
Xlibris
844-714-8691
www.Xlibris.com
Orders@Xlibris.com
834053

CONTENTS

FOREWORD

Many of you in the Christian community (who are also Motown fans) know that so much of today's music does not reflect the stirring, soulful music of Motown. As popular as that music was and still is, those of us who became Christians during that early era experienced a tremendous spiritual side of Motown that was not known to those on the outside.

I invite you to read these accounts of my spiritual journey included in this new book.

DEDICATION

This book is dedicated to God the Father, God the Son, and God the Holy Spirit; my dear husband Charles (now in heaven); and to Fay Hale (who passed on just prior to this book's publication), Brenda Boyce, Leila Glenn, Gloria Lennox, and all the prayer warriors at Motown who helped to pray signs and wonders (some that will only be revealed in heaven) in and over many people.

I also dedicate this book to my Pastors Scott and Phyllis Webb in Chelsea, Ala., for continuing to help me grow in the Word and in prayer. Thank you, Phyllis, for all you and Mrs. Peggy (Webb) have taught me – and continue to teach me – about the power of prayer.

To Beth Gray, who has helped me to edit this book – and taught me so much by the anointing of God on her life, assisting me in many areas where help was needed. I wish to thank Jean Bowick for lending her corrective pen to proofing and editing the manuscripts for printing. (Thanks Jean, you're a blessing.)

About the Author

Before she started working for Motown, Frances Levonia (Heard) Maclin was employed by the largest black-owned newspaper in Detroit, known then as *The Michigan Chronicle*. A Sales Associate in the *Classifieds* section, Frances procured the first ad for major retail giant, Woolworths Department Store, ever placed in a black Detroit newspaper.

While employed at Motown Records, Frances was affectionately known by her coworkers as Fran Heard Maclin. She worked for Motown for 25 years. During that time, she served as the Tape Librarian and was later promoted to Library Director, where she had the oversight of thousands of tapes recorded at Hitsville U.S.A. Studio; Golden World Studios; and MoWest Records, Motown's studio in Hollywood. These were Motown's main recording studios; however, there were other studios outside the company as well.

Frances had the awesome privilege of being part of almost every hit that was produced at Motown's main studios. She was the first one to handle a session reel after it left the control room.

Her job was to catalog and store each session reel, dispensing it back and forth between the engineer and producer until the songs were ready to be mixed – and finally (if selected) ready to be released.

During her years in the Tape Library, many songs that passed through Frances' hands went on to become No. 1 hits on the charts – *so* many that it would take several pages to name them all. However, "My Girl" by The Temptations and "I Hear A Symphony" by The Supremes are two of her favorites that nurtured from infancy to maturity.

Frances considered the Tape Library to be the bread and butter of the company. The duties of caring for the library were extensive. Many of the producers, to whom she gave a very hard time because they did *not* want to follow library rules (smile, Brian), probably appreciated the care and concern she took to ensure that these tapes were properly logged and documented.

Upon retiring from Motown in 1986, Frances joined her husband Charles in full-time ministry. She and Charles were married 41 years, until his passing in 2018. Frances now lives in Birmingham, Alabama, with her furry child Sebastian, a Cavalier King Charles Spaniel. Her first book, *I Remember Motown When We Were Just Family*, was published in 2010. It is available for purchase on Amazon.

CHANGED

In my first book, *I Remember Motown When We Were Just Family*, I write about Pops and Moms Gordy and my church attendance with them, both in Detroit and in California. I really believe the seed they sowed into my life regarding church propelled my desire to know the Lord more and to have a fuller relationship with Him.

Even though I had been in church every Sunday growing up, there was still a deep hunger for something more raging on the inside of me. Through a relationship with a past acquaintance, I walked down the aisle at Melodyland Christian Center in 1974 and gave my heart to Jesus. Immediately I became a new creature in Jesus Christ. "Therefore, if any man be in Christ, he is a new creature: old things are passed away; behold, all things are become new." (*2 Corinthians* 5:17)

All the years I had *religion* were now replaced with a real *relationship* with the Father God and the Lord Jesus Christ. I was saved!

Immediately I was changed. When I returned to work at Motown Studios the next day, I was no longer the Fran Heard who had left work the Friday before. Everything and everybody looked new to me. I was seeing through new eyes.

Neither my departmental head nor my supervisor, each of whom had been giving me a hard time at work, was able to provoke me to anger any longer – or to prod me into heated arguments that ended with yelling and swearing. Eventually they began to realize I was no longer the old Fran Heard, and they began to treat me differently. If they cursed, they apologized. If they argued, it was not with me.

I had many opportunities at Motown to walk in love and a *whole* lot of opportunities to perfect my love walk. I have many victorious testimonies because of my obedience and determination to walk in love with my coworkers.

Bible Study in the Car

When I transferred to Los Angeles from Detroit in 1972, I worked onsite at Motown Recording Studios. Later I moved to the main office on Sunset Boulevard and was shifted around several more times after that. These transitions were not peaceful times; I was in constant disagreement with my departmental head as well as my supervisor, and these disagreements were taking a toll on me.

During this time, I was introduced to Transcendental Meditation, a practice of Eastern religion in which followers meditate while silently repeating a mantra (a form of secret word). While participating in one of these sessions, I witnessed *my own feet levitating off the floor.*

After several of these meetings, I was talking more about Almighty God than the false Buddhist god I was supposed to be consulting. This made the people around me uncomfortable. It didn't take long for me to realize that Transcendental Meditation was not for me.

Not long after I left this group, a friend introduced me to the knowledge of salvation through Jesus Christ – something I knew absolutely nothing about. He invited me to attend a meeting at Melodyland Christian Center in nearby Anaheim. After I heard the message of salvation, I walked that long aisle to the altar and gave my life to Jesus in 1975. The empty hole in my heart was finally filled, and it has never been empty again.

After giving my life to the Lord, my hunger for the Word of God became an obsession. Because I had such a hunger for the Word, I spent my lunch hours in my car studying and reading God's Word, scriptures I was learning about in Bible study and church services. I always tried to park out of the sun to avoid the heat. The Lord was faithful – most of the time I found a space reserved just for me, just out of the sun.

It was my commitment to study and read the Bible that empowered me to be victorious on my job. I even experienced total victory over the persecution I had been receiving from those in authority over me.

THE BAPTISM OF
THE HOLY SPIRIT

In 1976 I decided to enroll in West Los Angeles Discipleship School to further grow my relationship with God. I recall telling Mr. Williams, my Angelology teacher at the school, that I needed to have the giants cast out of my life. I was referring to the challenges I faced daily at Motown after I got saved. It seemed to me that the devil was waiting for me to pull up in the parking lot every morning, and from the time I walked through the studio doors until I left for the day, I was in a spiritual battle.

Mr. Williams had been teaching our class about David and Goliath; he said we all face giants in our lives. When I told him about the giants at Motown, he looked at me with those piercing, yet kind, eyes and said, "You need to get filled with the Holy Ghost."

I didn't have the slightest idea who the Holy Ghost was. I belonged to a Methodist church and a Baptist Bible study – and neither of these denominations had taught me about the Holy

Ghost. Mr. Williams told me to come to the deliverance service that met once a week at his church and to talk with his wife. When I walked into that service, I found spiritual warfare at work! I was mesmerized with what I was seeing and hearing. In some parts of the room, I heard strange languages. In other parts I heard the words, "Come out in the name of Jesus!"

All over the room, strange things were happening. I didn't know what to do or think. Soon a very attractive lady came over to me. She had a peace on her face that was very apparent. She said to me, "I am Sister Williams, Brother Williams' wife. He told me about your hunger for God and that you want to have a deeper relationship with Him."

I talked to Sister Williams about my job, my family, and things I felt I needed to confess. She listened for about a minute, then said, "You've come to be baptized in the Holy Spirit. Begin to praise God; tell Him how much you love Him; lift up your hands to Him." Then she walked away.

I began to do what Sister Williams had instructed me to do, but my mind and my flesh were giving me a hard time. About ten minutes later, she returned to see how I was doing. I said, "Sister Williams, the devil is telling me I hate my mother." Then she said the strangest thing: "Tell the devil to shut up! Continue to praise God!"

So I lifted my hands again – and this time from my heart. I began to tell God how much I loved Him, and suddenly there was the most beautiful, indescribable light shining before me. I knew it was the presence of the Lord, and out of my belly began to flow strange words I never had spoken before.

Just then one of the counselors walked over to me and said, "Jesus is baptizing you in the Holy Ghost!" Oh, what a heavenly experience that was, rivers of living waters flowing out of me!

I knew that something extraordinary had happened to me. On my way to work after receiving my blessing, the joy of the Lord was all over me! When I arrived at the studio, I tried to explain to the ladies in the office what I had experienced. Of course, I couldn't explain it very well, but it was obvious to them that it was something very wonderful.

For my Evangelism meeting that night, we had a class assignment. We visited a private home and ministered to the family living there. One of the family members accepted Jesus and received salvation, and we prayed for another person who was sick.

After we left the house, one of my classmates asked me to give her a ride home. When I realized she lived in Inglewood (quite a distance from my apartment), I almost refused, but there was a boldness that had taken over me, and I knew I could do it. By the time we reached her house, however, a thick fog had rolled in, and I could barely see to find my way home.

As a driver I was accustomed to specific routes, so these weren't good conditions for me to travel in by myself. But I made it safely home with God's help. It was as if supernaturally, a big bus appeared suddenly on the road just ahead. I followed that bus all the way to my part of town where there was no fog. From there I drove home safely, under clear skies.

Soon after, I read a book on speaking in tongues. I knew I had to share it with my pastor. I called and told him about my new experience, being filled with the Holy Spirit. He said to me, "Now you have it all." I later learned that this spiritual gift was not embraced by the Methodist church, even though it was an early 20th-century Methodist preacher in California who led the Azuza Street Revival, a miraculous move of God which brought the baptism of the Holy Spirit to people all over the world.

After I was filled with the Holy Spirit with the evidence of speaking in other tongues, I became a totally different person. Even in my Christian infancy I knew that God loved me and He was on my side. I was no longer moved by the insults from my departmental head, and I could no longer be intimated by others. In other words, I had become a NEW WOMAN!

Angels Are Encamped Around Me

After I received Jesus as my personal Savior and the baptism of the Holy Ghost, I was not ashamed to present Him to anyone at Motown who would listen.

One morning I had the opportunity to share a personal testimony I shared on an elevator with several employees coming into work. Among them, the boss himself, Motown's founder Mr. Berry Gordy Jr.

I was the last one to get on the elevator that morning, and I jumped in praising the Lord, eager to share my testimony. As I was driving into work that day, it was raining steadily, and I was on a very slick road. I came out of a curve and lost control of my vehicle. My car began to spin, and I could not regain control.

Suddenly, I saw myself headed toward a parked car, and I knew I was in trouble. I was traveling on a busy street – usually cars were coming from the opposite direction. However, at that moment there was not another car in sight.

As I headed toward that parked car, it seemed that a supernatural force took over my driving! Within seconds of hitting that car, I came to complete stop just inches away from it. I had such a peace about the whole incident – I just backed my car up, headed it in the right direction and proceeded to work.

While I was putting my car in reverse, there wasn't another vehicle coming in either direction. I knew I had just had an encounter with an angel taking control of my vehicle. I blurted all of this out in the elevator that morning – I had a captive audience. I believe several people missed their floors just to hear the ending of my testimony.

Of course, my story got around. And once again, my peers knew I was serious about God and not ashamed to give Him Glory in my life.

Motown's Special Projects

After giving my life to the Lord, I was always seeking how to involve Motown in ways that would be pleasing to God. My department head did not agree with many of the projects I implemented, but the Spirit of the Lord would always convict him, so he had no choice but to allow me to do what was in my heart.

St. Elmo Village was one of my first projects. Cofounded by Rozzell Sykes and his nephew Roderick in 1969, St. Elmo Village is a public art community in Mid City L.A. that transformed a neighborhood block into an artistic experiment. The houses were colorfully painted, the sidewalks covered with drawings – and the back of his house was full of all kinds of elaborate sculptures crafted from discarded metal scraps, bottles, you name it. I named it – and I called it extraordinary.

However, after getting to know Rozzell, I knew the Lord had led me to this Village for a reason. I visited the Village on many occasions and shared the Lord with Rozzell and his family. He knew I worked for Motown, and he wanted to show his artwork to some of our label's musical artists. I couldn't *promise* him that he'd be able to show his work at Motown; however, I did invite many people to come see his Village.

In addition, Motown studio personnel helped me put together Easter baskets for the children at St. Elmo's, and what a blessing they were. I got to share with their families the real meaning of Easter. Although I never heard Rozzell confess Jesus Christ as his Lord and Savior, I *knew* I had sown good seed into his life and mission. In appreciation to my coming to the Village, Rozzell made a Bible sculpture for me that I kept for many years. He also went on to create murals in one of the tunnels of downtown L.A.

Teaming with Rozzell, we completed a Thanksgiving project for the Village, during which we gave away turkeys and Thanksgiving baskets to needy families. As part of our Christmas project, we gave toys and gifts to underprivileged families. These were all behind-the-scene gestures that most people knew nothing about. Motown clearly had a heart for music – and a soul of love for so many less fortunate.

HAL Awards with prayer partners Fay Hale and Brenda Boyce

Our Wedding - August 27, 1977

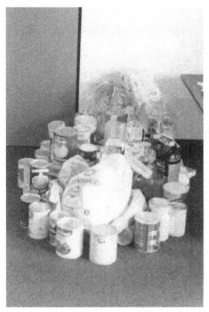 

Getting staples ready for needy families

Stan Broder (middle) helping with St. Elmo's Basket

Thanksgiving meals for needy families

Christmas gifts for needy kids

Rozelle Sykes with St. Elmo's kids

The Maclin Family

Motown's First Prayer Closet

As more and more of my coworkers (especially those who had been my friends in Detroit) got saved, we knew the Lord had a plan for us at Motown. We began to seek the Lord as to how He desired us to be a witness for Him. The Lord revealed to me the necessity to begin praying for Mr. Gordy and the company as a whole. Thus began the first Motown prayer group.

There were four of us who started that prayer group. The first thing we had to do was to find a place to pray. Leila Glen, one of our prayer partners, was secretary to Motown's executive vice-president and had a storage closet in her area. Leila said she would ask her boss if we could use it for prayer. We knew we'd have to support her in prayer about this because her boss was Jewish and definitely not a Christian believer. So we prayed in faith, believing, and the Lord touched her boss's heart – he allowed us to use that closet for our prayer group meetings.

As I recall, I had two specific ministries attached to the prayer group. When our group first started meeting, I set out flyers in some of the office suites Motown was renting in our Sunset Boulevard location. I didn't ask permission before I distributed the flyers, however, so I was called on the carpet by our very own CEO, Mr. Berry Gordy IV. He said it wasn't wise for me to circulate Christian flyers in the office since so many of our coworkers held contrary religious beliefs. I understood his concern, and I asked his forgiveness for distributing the flyers without his permission.

The Lord had touched Mr. Gordy's heart, however, so he gave me permission to have the prayer group anyway with those who'd responded to our flyers. As I was leaving his office that day, I noticed that he had a severe cold. I asked him if I could pray for him, and he said yes! As I laid my hands on Mr. Gordy and prayed for his divine healing, I sensed the power of God flowing into his body. I *knew* that he had been helped. When I left his office, he thanked me for praying. God was at work!

Over the next few months, our group really began to grow; we knew we would need a larger place to meet. Before long, Fay Hale, another one of our prayer partners, offered us a small room available in her office area. It was the ideal setting, as it gave us the opportunity to grow – and grow we did!

Eventually we outgrew that room too, and it was then that I met Esther Kim, property manager of the Sunset Boulevard building. Kim was a Spirit-filled Chinese Christian who loved the Lord. She was so happy to know we had a prayer group meeting at Motown. She offered us an empty office to use for our prayer time. We met for several weeks in that Sunset office. We knew this place was an answer to prayer.

The enemy, however, was not happy with the growth of our group. Slowly the devil began to infiltrate our meetings. Some of our newer "religious" members brought with them gossip, strife, and vain chatter. Ultimately, I realized it was time to shut down this particular group, since it was no longer accomplishing what the Lord had raised it up to be.

We still had our core group, however, and the Lord began to work mightily through us as we stayed faithful to His purpose.

We began a tract outreach on Hollywood Boulevard, passing out gospel tracts by the hundreds to all kinds of personalities. During one of our outreach campaigns, Fay Hale was approached by a man who berated her for handing out Bible tracts on the street corner. He told her she was a very attractive woman, but she looked like a fool standing out there handing out those tracts to complete strangers. Fay told that man she considered it an honor to be called a fool for Jesus!

During our ministry on Hollywood Boulevard, we had the opportunity to pray with many people and invite them to church. But most importantly, we were able to let people know Jesus *loved* them – no matter who they were or what they'd done – just by handing them a gospel tract about the Lord and His infinite grace.

During our tenure, God gave our Bible study group a variety of outreach assignments. Our biggest task was to evangelize our entire Sunset Boulevard building – all 20 floors – through our gospel tract ministry. God gave us the exact plan: we were to place tracts in every bathroom on all 20 floors.

We were like secret agents infiltrating enemy territory. On the day of our mission, we arrived at work around 7 a.m., spent time in prayer, then began our individual assignments.

This was such an exciting time! Each of us was responsible for specific floors, and we had to finish *all* floors before 9 a.m. Last on my list were the executive suites on the 20th floor. To my dismay, however, access to these restrooms required a key, which I didn't have. Thankfully, God was on the scene! The cleaning crew happened to be working on that floor, and at just the right moment, one of the crew members passed through the executive doorway. No one in that crew knew I didn't work on that floor, so when they saw me there, they simply left the door open for me to enter. PRAISE THE LORD!

I immediately went to each restroom after the cleaning crew finished up. I laid out my tracts in the executive bathrooms and even hit a few of the offices on the way out. I felt so good, like a special agent on divine assignment from the Lord.

Once we had covered all floors, we reconvened in Fay's office. Rejoicing together, we shared our adventures – and we were back at our own desks to begin work by 9 a.m. God's perfect timing!

I can't end this chapter without mentioning some of the people whose lives the Lord allowed us personally to influence. One of our vice presidents, a Jewish man who had been staunchly opposed to our group's Christian outreach ministry, asked us to pray for him when he was diagnosed with cancer. Brenda Boyce, then Motown's creative director, ministered to Grammy-nominated recording artist Teena Marie, who at that time was going through some difficult personal challenges. Brenda was able to persuade Teena to attend some of our church services, where she heard God's Word and received the help she needed from the Lord.

Motown also had a new artist (whose name I won't reveal) in desperate need of godly counsel. She was a beautiful young woman with tremendous talent and a gorgeous body, and she was using *both* to gain auditions with record producers. Fay Hale ministered *life* to this young lady. This budding, beautiful star received God's Word; turned her life over to Jesus; and has since become a positive, public witness for the Lord.

Once I personally ministered to a female coworker in our finance department. In my office I had some beautiful Christian posters on the walls, most of which included a scripture. Because this sweet lady could tell I was a Christian, she would come over to talk with me at my desk. She was so impressed with my posters because they were such a positive influence. My departmental head was not thrilled that my Christian posters were prominently displayed in the office – however, he wasn't bold enough to ask me to take them down.

One day when my coworker was visiting me, she said, "I want what *you* have, Frances. You are so peaceful, and you seem not to allow anything to bother you – how do you do it?"

I began to talk to this young lady about Jesus and how my life changed when I accepted Him as my Savior and Lord. I told her that He could help her too. I led her in the sinner's prayer of salvation (based on Romans Chapter 8). Right then she accepted Jesus as her Savior, and her entire countenance changed before my very eyes! I encouraged her to join a good church right away where the pastor teaches faith and preaches the Word of God. I told her I would love to have her visit my church. For a whole season I drove across town every Sunday to pick up this sweet lady and her children to take them to church. It was well worth the drive. The lives of this young lady and her precious family were forever changed.

We were blessed with many opportunities to share Jesus with our coworkers and Motown recording artists who readily received our ministry. We are confident that many of those who heard our message will meet us in heaven one day. To God be all the glory!

BIBLE STUDY IN HOLLYWOOD HILLS

Frank Wilson, who passed away several years ago, was a singer, songwriter, and one of Motown's top producers. When I moved from Detroit to Los Angeles, I had no idea that two years later, our paths would cross as new creatures in Christ.

As I began my walk with the Lord, I began to hear about a weekly Bible study Frank was having in his home in the Hollywood Hills. When I finally touched base with Frank, I asked him if it would be okay to attend the study. He welcomed me with open arms.

I remember the first Bible study I attended at Frank's home. I went with a friend, and we wound up getting lost on the way there, as I was not used to driving in the Hills. Thankfully, the Holy Spirit was my co-driver. We finally managed to find the house – and what a house it was, sitting way on top of the mountain! I remember wondering how in the world I was going to get down from there.

dies were very interesting. For the first time I saw
people were to know the Word of God. There was
of celebrities there, including songwriters and movie
ong with regular folks like me who came to hear the
aught. We were wide open to receive.

nded several of Frank's Bible studies and eventually became
rayer partner with his wife Bunny. I really valued Bunny's
iendship; she was totally sold out to the Lord. Because she
loved me, she told me that fornication was a sin, and that I
needed to sever the relationship I was in. It took a while for me
to become convicted by the Holy Spirit that I truly *was* in sin.
In my apartment one evening, I became convicted. I asked the
Lord to forgive me, and out of my innermost being came this
pronouncement, "I have decided to follow Jesus."

I couldn't wait to tell Bunny I was free! I had become a regular
at Frank's Bible study, and one day I introduced him to the
director of the Discipleship School I was attending. This school
was reaching across denominations and bringing young people
together who were hungry for God.

This was a divine connection. Frank asked the director to
teach many of the Bible study lessons, helping bring those in
attendance to a higher spiritual level. The Bible study, however,
eventually ran its course. By the direction of the Holy Spirit,
Frank knew when it was time to close it down. Those of us who
attended those Bible studies were greatly blessed by them; we
had grown so much from the teachings we received there.

Psalm 91

Psalm 91:10-12 reads: "There shall no evil befall thee, neither shall any plague come nigh thy dwelling. For he shall give his angels charge over thee to keep thee in thy in all ways. They shall bear thee up in their hands, lest thou dash thy foot against a stone."

What started out as an incredible evening at Discipleship School turned into a night I shall never forget. We had just finished a series of good teaching on discipleship, and on my drive home I was basking in what I had been taught.

Since I had driven directly from work to school, I hadn't eaten dinner yet, so I stopped at a fast-food restaurant to pick up a burger and fries. As I continued home, I was caught up in praising the Lord for the wonderful time of praise, worship, and teaching we had just enjoyed at school.

At my apartment complex, I pulled into the parking area and got out of my car. When I opened the back door and leaned inside to get my books, a man came up behind me in an instant. He stuck a gun in my back and ordered me to get in the passenger seat of my car. "I'll kill you if you scream," he threatened as he climbed into the driver's seat.

You would think I would've been petrified at this moment. However, the peace of God that passes all understanding dropped all over me! I said to the man, "I'm not going to scream – I'm going to obey you." I had just read Hebrews 13:7 in my daily scripture reading that said, "Obey them that have the rule over you. . ."!

As the man drove my car down the service road past my apartment building, my mind tried to understand what was happening. But it just wouldn't process.

The stranger – the man driving my car, pointing a gun at me – asked if I was married. I said, "Yes," though my marriage at that time was to the Lord Jesus. My kidnapper threatened me again, saying, "If you try to jump out this car, I'll kill you!"

"You can lay the gun down," I reassured him, "I am going to obey you." As we sped past familiar landmarks toward a place still unknown to me, the peace that covered me created an atmosphere in the car that relaxed even the kidnapper.

We came to a very dark area with several alleyways, and the man finally chose an alley to enter. I knew then that it was his intent to rape me. Under my breath I whispered, "Lord, you said you would never leave me or forsake me" (Hebrews 13:5).

I didn't know how, but I *knew* God was going to deliver me! The man stopped behind a building and ordered me to climb into the back seat. Pointing a gun at me, he ordered me to take off my undergarments. Without going into graphic detail, I explained to him that I was dealing with some female issues and asked him not to hurt me. I don't know exactly what he was thinking, but this thought appalled him. As an alternative, he ordered me to commit oral sex with him.

I told the man I didn't have any idea what he was talking about. I was completely surrendered to the Holy Spirit – God was speaking through my lips. Finally, the man asked me in disgust, "How do you and your husband make love?!"

From out of my mouth came these words: "We allow the Lord to help us in our lovemaking." Astonished, he looked at me and said, "Either you are the biggest liar, or you are telling the truth!"

The kidnapper ordered me out of the car. He told me he was taking my car, but I *would* get it back. He allowed me to take all my personal belongings with me, and he even gave me bus fare to get home, which I kept for several years.

I don't have full revelation regarding my reason for doing this, but before the man left, I asked him if I could kiss him on the cheek. He asked me why; I said it was just something I needed to do. Today I recall his countenance – the face of my would-be rapist – changing right before my eyes. Then he ordered me to stay in the alley until he drove away.

I am fully persuaded that my angel was right there protecting me the whole time. As Genesis 48:16 says, "The Angel which redeemed me from all evil" kept me safe from harm.

The next thing I recall is knocking on the door of my friend Vivian's house, several blocks from where I was taken. I don't remember walking those blocks. Like Philip the Evangelist (Acts 8:39), God must have picked me up and carried me away. When Vivian opened the door, there I stood with my books and tape recorder in my hands, and all I could say was, "Vivian, God has delivered me from the hands of a rapist! We must pray!"

Vivian began to cry, and both of us fell on our faces and began to intercede in prayer for that man. I believe that when I get to heaven one day, he will be there too.

After we finished praying, Vivian encouraged me to report the incident to the police. We rode down to our local police precinct, and I related the full account of my assault to the officer on duty. When the policeman tried to pull up my driver's license, however, it wasn't there! He decided to take us back to the briefing room so they could record my story.

Remarkably, the person who took my statement was a lady named Jay – an old friend of mine from Detroit. That night the whole station crew listened to my amazing testimony. When my friend finished recording my story, she told me she would stay in touch. As we were leaving the precinct, the first young officer we'd met told us he had decided to get back into church. Praise the Lord for what He was beginning!

When I got back to my apartment, I realized my door key was still on the keychain with my car keys. So I walked over to the complex office and told my story to the night security officer, who was as stunned as the police department was. He kindly walked me back to my apartment and instructed me to bolt the door.

By that time I was so exhausted, I could hardly wait to get to bed. I was asleep for what felt like a few minutes when I was awakened by loud, forceful pounding on my door. When I asked who it was, an authoritative voice answered, "OPEN UP, THIS IS THE POLICE!"

When I opened the door, there stood several law enforcement officers with their hands on their weapons. The officer in charge asked me if anyone else was in the apartment. I told him no, I lived alone. He requested my permission to search the apartment, which of course I gave. Finally, I asked how they had gotten my address, since my car had been stolen.

As it turned out, the man who had kidnapped me earlier in the evening had just kidnapped and raped another woman.

Because the attacker had been driving my car, the woman he raped had seen my license plate and given my plate number to the police. *This* turned out to be the reason my license information was not accessible at the precinct earlier – my records had been pulled by another precinct because of this new rape report.

Once again I related the story of my kidnapping, which astonished these officers as well. It also gave me another opportunity to witness to them about God's goodness and how He protects his people. When those officers left my apartment that night, they knew I had just experienced a miracle in my life. Some of them said, "You're a lucky girl." But I said, "No, I am a *blessed* girl."

The policemen asked me to contact the detective division at the local precinct the next day to give them my statement regarding the new developments. I called my departmental head at Motown that morning and related my story to him, and of course he was in awe as well. I told him I probably would not be at work that day since I had to go back to the police station to complete my interview, and I still had not had any rest.

When I returned to the police precinct, the detective asked me to retell my experience with the attacker. By that time, I could relate the incident backward and forward. Once again, I saw complete amazement in his face. He kept asking me if I had been raped, so I kept saying, "No!"

Finally, the detective told me what had happened to the woman who had been raped. She had been waiting at the bus stop when the man pulled up in my car and threatened her with the gun. He ordered her into the passenger seat, then took her to a secluded place and raped her. The detective asked me for a detailed description of the man and had me look at pictures of known rapists on file.

None of the men in the photos looked like my kidnapper. However, the officer said he would stay in touch, and let me know when they turned up any leads. He also gave me the name and number of the woman who was raped. He thought perhaps I could be of some encouragement to her.

When I called the woman, I told her I was the lady whose car had been stolen and used in her attack. She asked if the rapist had threatened me; I told her that he had. She then wanted to know if he had raped me too. I told her no. In a sudden, startled outburst, she asked me, "*Why?*"

The only way I knew to answer her rightly was to tell her exactly what had happened to me. She said, "*I'm* a Christian. My father is a pastor. Why *me?*" My heart went out to this woman because I knew the difference in our situation – why she was raped and I wasn't. It was because I had stepped out on God's Word in faith, and she hadn't.

As time went on, I tried to keep in touch with the woman and keep her encouraged. One day I called, however, and her phone had been disconnected. I called the detective who was in charge of case; he said she had gone back home to her family because the trauma of the rape had been very hard on her. I was sad to hear this because I had such a desire to help her.

As time passed, I continued to believe my car would be recovered, and sure enough, it was. My friend Jay, with whom I had been reunited at the police station, found my car at a police impound yard.

Jay wasn't supposed to give me this information because impound protocol was to keep recovered vehicles for a certain amount of time before notifying the owners. This strategy was designed to allow the yard to collect larger recovery fees from daily impound charges – the longer the impound lot kept your car, the more money they charged you.

Naturally the impound man was surprised to see us so soon after my car was located. It had just been brought into the lot. He didn't seem happy at all that we were there to claim the car; he wanted to know *who* had informed us that my vehicle was on the impound lot. I tried to share with him the testimony of my kidnapping and deliverance, but this man just wasn't interested. He was looking for dollars!

My friend Bill, who had brought me to the impound yard, was a devoted, God-fearing man who had the love of God oozing out of him. He started talking with the keeper of the yard, and before long, the Spirit of God had melted that man's heart. He allowed me to take my car right out of the lot – without any additional charges – and wished me well.

I didn't see my friend Jay again after she called me about the car. She left that position at the police department soon after. As I reflect over this period in time, I wonder, was she there just for me? Did God have her in that position specifically to be a blessing to me (as well as to others)? The answer is *Yes*! I also believe that in seeing her again, I had an opportunity to share important truths with her about the Gospel that may have helped turn her life around too.

Over the years I've had the opportunity to be a witness for Jesus to people all over the world, sharing my testimony with one person at a time – or when I spoke on Trinity Broadcasting Network (TBN), *millions* at a time. I believe that over the next 30-or-more years, my God-given testimony will continue to glorify the amazing power of God to all those who believe!

My Wedding Day

As I reflect back to the day Charles and I were married in a small, Los Angeles Baptist church in 1977, I remember the many Motown stars, coworkers and friends in attendance.

Our finances were very limited then, so we had to believe God every step of the way. I had to believe God for our rings, our flowers for the church, my wedding dress, our reception hall, and money for our honeymoon. We were so challenged financially that I also asked the Lord to help by providing the food I desired for our reception.

I'd remembered a very special cake that one of my good friends, Gwen Patrick, had served at her wedding. It was homemade with several layers, and it was truly unique. I contacted the lady who made it and asked her to make one for me. She agreed to make it for a very small price. As we got closer to my wedding date, however, the lady had an emergency. She would need to be out of town when my wedding day arrived.

Still, I had my heart set on that cake! I asked her if I could freeze the cake if she made it ahead of time. She said yes, the cake would be just as good, even frozen. Now, I didn't have the slightest idea where I would find a place to store the cake until our wedding. Thank God for the LeDeauxs. They had a small restaurant with a large walk-in freezer, and they agreed to store my cake for me. God is so good! They not only stored our wedding cake, they also catered my bridal rehearsal dinner with fish, chicken and gumbo – completely free of charge.

God also led me to ask the good cooks at our church to provide one dish each. My, how He did spread the table! The only dish I was missing was a relish tray. Then, on the day of the wedding, one of the largest relish trays I had ever seen arrived at the hall where our reception was to be held. It was from Beverly Hills, courtesy of Gwen Gordy Fuqua, sister of Berry Gordy Jr.

All of my table arrangements were made by one of my classmates from the discipleship school where I attended. My coworker and his wife had a very large flower garden, so I asked them to provide the flowers for the church. When I arrived at the church, there were large professional baskets of flowers all around the altar. He and his wife had decided to have a florist provide the flowers as a wedding gift to us.

My bridesmaids were my girlfriends who had come all the way from Detroit, with the exception of Claudette Robinson and Jo Moxely, who lived in California. The groomsmen were the deacons from our church. I also had a large company of other friends who came from Detroit to California to be part of my special day.

My best friend Willie Ruth McGee (now in heaven) helped me get dressed to walk down the aisle. She and I were using one of the back rooms of the church as a dressing room, when suddenly the spirit of worship fell on us, so we just basked in the glory of God! It felt like I was literally flowing down the aisle to be forever married to the man Charles Curtis Maclin, whom the Lord had brought into my life.

There were so many other matrimonial miracles besides the ones I have noted! It was just like God the Father to give his daughter the very best wedding ever!

Laid Off

During the late 1970s the company experienced some financial difficulties, so many departments at Motown were asked to lay off some of their employees for a short period of time. In my department I had more seniority than anyone else.

I was also the only one whose job could not be duplicated.

Much to my surprise, however, my departmental head chose me to lay off. What he said (in so many words), was that because of my stand on honesty and truth, I would not be of assistance to him. Right away I knew what he meant – I wouldn't lie or cover up anything "questionable" regarding studio operations.

I responded by telling my departmental head that although I was being laid off, he could feel free to call me if he needed me, and I would come in to work without pay. Naturally this caught him completely off guard, and he was speechless.

While I was out of work, I continued to pay my tithes and give offerings to the church, even though I had no income. God was supplying my needs supernaturally.

I remember one incident in particular. During my prayer time, I felt impressed to take a bag of groceries to a couple who had come into some hard times. They were both actors and had come to Los Angeles Christian Center after hearing Pastor Floyd C. Miller on the radio. They weren't married, but they had a hunger for God.

After praying that morning, I checked my finances. To my surprise, I had enough money to buy this couple some groceries. I immediately went shopping and was able to put together a good meal for them.

I knew the couple lived in Hollywood, but exactly where, I was unsure. So, I got in my car and drove up to the part of town where I thought they might live. From that point, I depended on the Holy Spirit to lead me, and He did!

I pulled up in front of an apartment building, and I knew on the inside that this was the right building. I walked up to the mailboxes, and sure enough, there were their names, Julie and Will. I rang the doorbell. Julie came to the door, and her entire countenance changed. She grabbed me and hugged me, and I hugged her. I told her about my time in prayer and how I was led to come there and bring them food. Tears of joy bubbled up in her, because their refrigerator was empty!

Praise the Lord! This gesture of love pulled her and Will even closer to the church. I am happy to report that they went on to get married, and when we left Los Angeles Christian Center in 1986, they were still serving the Lord.

A short time after being obedient to the Lord in this way, I received a phone call from someone in the payroll department at Motown. She told me we were going to be called back into work and to wait on a call.

After waiting several days, however, I still had not received a call from my departmental head, even though I knew of others who already had been called back to work. I finally decided to call him myself. His response to me was, "You're never coming back."

I knew it was not time for me to leave Motown, so I sought the Lord for the next step to take. I was led to call the secretary of our senior vice president, who was also one of our prayer partners; I shared with her what my departmental head had said to me. She agreed to pass on the information to the senior VP.

A few hours later, I received a phone call from my departmental head's secretary. She said I was to report back to work Monday morning.

My prayer partner told me later on that after she told the senior VP about my conversation with the departmental head, he almost hit the ceiling. He had her place a phone call to my departmental head, and he gave my departmental head a chewing-out that included lots of language she couldn't repeat.

She did tell me one thing the senior VP said during that conversation, however, that bode well for me: "How in the *world* are you going to fire someone who has more seniority than you *and* who started out with Mr. Gordy at the very beginning of the company? *And* who knows more about the Tape Library than you'll ever know?" This was the crux of the conversation. It also was the favor of God – His favor that got my job back and continued to work for me at Motown until the day I retired.

Stan Broder's Conversion

Stan was one of my supervisors at Motown Studios. He was Jewish and remarkably knowledgeable about his Jewish roots and his covenant with God. Although he did not actively *practice* his religion, anytime I tried to witness to him about Jesus, he was quick to remind me of his heritage.

I knew that Stan was not a happy man; he tried practicing all the things he thought might give him peace. My born-again experience bought us closer together, even though he would not listen to me when I talked about Jesus.

One day he told me he was going to quit work and visit some Far Eastern countries. As much as he would listen, I talked to him about Jesus. One day I blurted out to him, "Stan, if you don't get saved, you are going to die and go to hell!"

Saying this did not leave me in good standing with Stan. When he got ready to leave the States, he called me and said he would write to me, but he did not want me to mention Jesus to him.

I agreed; however, I did not keep my word, because I would always end my letters by saying, "Jesus loves you."

After several letters, Stan began to mention various people he had met during his travels, and most of them were Christians. In one of his letters, he asked me if I was *praying* for Christians to be put in his path; I am sure that I was.

Stan was gone for several months. One day as I was sitting in my car, reading my Bible in the studio parking lot, I heard a voice saying, "Hello, Sister." I recognized the voice, but the words themselves were a big surprise. I looked up, and it was Stan! The first words out of my mouth were, "Stan, you got saved!"

Stan went on to share with me that while he was in the Middle East, he was in a Turkish dope den, a place where they smoked hashish from pipe bowls. He smoked too much, and based on his reaction to it, he knew he was dying. The only thing he could remember was calling out to Jesus, "Jesus, if you are real, help me!"

When Stan woke up, he was aware that Jesus had saved his life. He began to make his way back to the U.S., and the Lord put Christians in his path all the way back. His testimony to them was that his black sister in Los Angeles had told him if he didn't receive Jesus as Savior, he would die and go to hell. Of course, I was surprised to know that he was including me in his testimony of being saved, but I was glad he did.

Stan continued to grow in his walk with the Lord. He began duplicating taped sermons for a large Christian ministry which took him to many countries. I am sure that at this writing he is still involved in the things of the Lord.

I had an opportunity to fellowship with Stan not long before he graduated to heaven in 2017. He was still very involved with his church and very much in love with the Lord. I am so proud to have called Stan my born-again Jewish brother.

JACK

Jack was one of our disc lathe engineers, a stressful job at Motown. He was Jewish, and we had a good coworkers' relationship. We usually talked about what he was working on and events pertaining to the company.

One particular day, Jack and I were talking in the lathe room. I don't remember our topic of conversation, but it turned towards the Bible. As we talked, I sensed that Jack was interested in spiritual things; everything he referred to was centered around the Old Testament.

The more Jack and I talked, the more I realized he did not understand that Jesus had died for him and had paid the price for his sins. I began to share with him that the blood of animals could no longer cover his sins because animal sacrifices were no longer being done. Jack was not attending a synagogue at that time, but I knew he believed that his people were chosen of God. As I shared more with him about Jesus' being the sacrificial lamb for our sins today, I could tell that light was beginning to dawn in him.

Jack and I had many conversations about the Bible over the years. I had opportunities to pray with him about situations involving his work, his family, and other concerns. I did not personally lead him to Christ, but I sowed good spiritual seeds into him. I believe that someone else came along to water those seeds, that God gave the increase, and that I'll see Jack again in heaven one day.

REFLECTIONS

Christmastime

For several years when we lived in California, we would visit Smokey Robinson's family every Christmas Eve and have a time of warm fellowship with them. We spent this time around the Word of God and reflecting on the goodness of God. We always enjoyed these special times with them.

We would leave the Robinsons' home to visit with the Colemans (Berry the IV, Terry, and Hazel Gordy's grandparents). Mr. and Mrs. Coleman always welcomed our visits, as it also gave us the opportunity to minister the Word of God to them and show them the love of Jesus.

Loucye Gordy Wakefield's Memorial Observances

For several years after Mr. Gordy's sister Loucye (Lou, as we called her) passed away, the family observed the anniversary of her passing. At her cemetery plot there was usually a song, a scripture reading, and remarks from the family. I was always blessed to write an inspirational piece to be read. This was such an honor for me because Mom Gordy always depended on me to write a fitting piece that spoke of the tremendous legacy that Lou left behind.

Visit With Little Stevie Wonder

I had an opportunity to visit Little Stevie Wonder's home just after he signed with Motown. What a delight it was to meet his mother Lula and his siblings. I could tell there was never a dull moment in that house. Stevie as usual was the center of attention and kept us royally entertained. Of course, Stevie went on to record and sell millions of records. I wrote about him in my first book, *I Remember Motown (When We Were Just Family)*.

Tina Marie

We were so blessed to have Tina Marie visit our church, Los Angeles Christian Center, on several occasions. She was very well received by our pastor, Dr. Floyd C. Miller, and the members of our congregation. We were able to share the Word of God with her and pray with her regarding some challenges she was having. She came to the church several times, and I know we were a big help to her. I'm sure she and Dr. Miller have reflected on these times, as they are both now in heaven together. I have so much that I could reflect on. Perhaps in another book, I'll be able to share even more.

Watching the Sunset from the 14th Floor

Working at Motown in California, every day had special challenges. Perhaps we had received the wrong tape for a recording session or encountered an irate producer whose session was delayed. Our storage facility may have called to tell us an important tape had been misplaced, or Mr. Gordy asked me to retrieve a particular tape recorded at the studio years earlier.

With all the challenges of working at Motown, my favorite time of day was watching the sunset from the 14th floor. I always knew the end of the workday would be coming soon, and my sunset would reassure me that all was well; God had accomplished through me the winning of every challenge for that day.

Each afternoon, as the sun began its descension over the Hollywood Hills, I would watch the Holy Spirit paint the most beautiful landscape across the sky. The colors were extraordinary and totally breathtaking. I would sit in my chair looking out through the window, knowing that God was performing this display especially for me.

Once the sun was set and the celestial art show was over, I would look around my office to see the work that would greet me when I returned to the office the next morning. I would then thank God for that day and for the magnificent sunset that sealed it. And I would know that another beautiful sunset would be waiting for me again tomorrow.

CPSIA information can be obtained
at www.ICGtesting.com
Printed in the USA
JSHW021650110423
40201JS00001B/3